D0911087

From the Prize Ring to the Pulpit

ONE MAN'S JOURNEY TO A LIFETIME OF FAITH

Carolyn Rhame Kelley

WESTBOW
PRESS®
A DIVISION OF THOMAS NELSON
& ZONDERVAN

WestBow Press books may be ordered through booksellers or by contacting:

WestBow Press
A Division of Thomas Nelson & Zondervan
1663 Liberty Drive
Bloomington, IN 47403
www.westbowpress.com
1 (866) 928-1240

Because of the dynamic nature of the Internet, any web addresses or
links contained in this book may have changed since publication and
may no longer be valid. The views expressed in this work are solely those
of the author and do not necessarily reflect the views of the publisher,
and the publisher hereby disclaims any responsibility for them.

Any people depicted in stock imagery provided by Thinkstock are
models, and such images are being used for illustrative purposes only.
Certain stock imagery © Thinkstock.

ISBN: 978-1-5127-2744-9 (sc)
ISBN: 978-1-5127-2745-6 (hc)
ISBN: 978-1-5127-2743-2 (e)

Library of Congress Control Number: 2016900871

Print information available on the last page.

WestBow Press rev. date: 1/28/2016

Contents

Acknowledgments

U PON RETIRING FROM TEACHING A few years ago, I started writing inspirational devotionals called *Lunch at the Park* for my church's women's ministry. At the same time, I also started writing morning devotionals for my daughter Laurie's high school classroom at Little Rock Christian Academy, titled *Mondays with Mom*. While I had been privileged to coauthor a couple of articles for publications during my tenure on the faculties of Southeast Missouri State University and the University of Central Arkansas, the thought of writing a book seemed daunting. As I shared this thought, former colleagues of mine at the University of Central Arkansas, Drs. Ann Witcher and Patty Phelps; my pastor's wife, Nancy Greer; and my longtime friend Cathy Cheek; encouraged me to continue writing. I am grateful for the opportunity that Laurie and Nancy afforded me in writing and also for the reassurance and friendship of my former colleagues and Cathy.

From the first time I was old enough to understand Dad's story, I have been intrigued; and so six months before he passed away in 1986, I sat down in a series of interviews and taped his story to preserve for my brother, Paul, his family, and mine. Over the years I sometimes would retrieve the tape to relive Dad's voice and story and then put it aside. I never gave thought to writing his story until after I had retired from the university in 2007. Little by little I began putting various thoughts together and writing a portion of his story; most of my time, however, was taken up with the care of my precious mother whose health had begun deteriorating, and I put the story aside once again.

In the fall of 2013, after Mother had passed away, I felt an extreme urgency to complete what I had started several years ago. Since writing Dad's story was to be a surprise for the family, I did not seek to have my manuscript edited for publication. My goal was to share and touch their hearts with Dad's remarkable life. Indeed it did. Upon receiving his copy of Dad's story, my nephew, Tim, called immediately to let me know that this story needed to be published. He, along with my son Greg, and my daughters, Laurie and Sarah, pushed me to write this book.

Although I knew the story well from the many times Dad shared it from various pulpits throughout the years, I have spent countless hours going over the interview. With notes in hand, I researched the proper spelling of the names of people he told about from the early thirties. I tried to find articles but had little success, although I did find one from the time he fought for the lightweight championship of East Tennessee. Unfortunately, he did not keep the many newspaper clippings from his days as a prizefighter and entertainer, often throwing each away when it became old news to him or tattered from carrying the article in his wallet. How I wish he had kept these!

During the time Mother lived with us, I had the wonderful opportunity of reading Dad's love letters to her and combing through scrapbooks, both hers and mine. For months, I prayed over this as I wrote his story, reread, and revised countless times in trying to convey the many facets of his life that led to his ministry and his tremendous love for the Lord.

Adding to this undertaking has been my dear brother, Paul Rhame, who, over the past months, has read and reread and assisted me in editing as we went over parts of this book. He has also refreshed my memory of stories not on tape. His years of teaching English in an all-boys college-preparatory high school has helped me wade through forgotten, pesky grammar rules to make me a better writer. I can think of no better person to walk with me through this journey. Thank you, Paul. Our times together have been priceless, and I am so grateful for our loving relationship. I owe you a heart of gratitude.

I would be remiss if I did not thank my husband of fifty-two years. Throughout our lifetime together, Ted has been my ardent supporter in encouraging me in everything I have attempted to do. I am grateful for his willingness to afford me the hours it takes to write. Thank you for your love!

Finally, without the saving power of Jesus Christ, this book could not have been written. There is no amount of gratitude I can offer that can match His love and grace.

Introduction

THE BOY RUNS UP THE flight of stairs until he reaches the second floor and peers over the balcony. The students have gathered for another school assembly. He tosses a piece of chalk up into the air and rushes back down the stairs, hoping to take a seat before the chalk hits the floor. It is a game. His hopes of not getting caught are dashed as a teacher grabs his arm and marches him to the principal's office. Once again, his mother will be summoned to the school. What do you do with a boy who can't sit still; who twists his hair with one hand while biting his nails down to the quick on the other hand; who makes straight A's in everything except conduct because he can't keep his feet from swinging in constant motion; and who is bright and gifted?

It is sometime around 1917, and the boy is seven-years-old. During this time, the organized study of child development was in its infancy, and teachers were not encouraged to search the backgrounds of students to gain a better understanding of their behaviors. The delivery of information was generally a lecture, and a child was expected to sit still and be quiet for long periods.

Today's terms, such as attention deficit disorder (ADD), attention-deficit hyperactivity disorder (ADHD), or gifted were not in educators' vocabularies. Learning styles weren't even considered, and Howard Gardner's multiple intelligences were far from being theorized. Neither were there school counselors to offer recommendations or insight. This boy would have to struggle alone with issues that a child should not have to face.

If there had been an investigation into the background of this elementary student, the school would have learned of the abuse that permeated his home life, abuse so severe that it caused a young boy to behave in ways that—in educated circles of today's understanding—would help to explain the extreme nervousness and restless nature. They would also have understood that the restlessness came from being hungry many times and that there was no recourse but to remain hungry. This young boy's story cuts into my heart and penetrates my every emotion because the boy was my dad, and the abuser, my grandfather.

1

A Boyhood Less Desired

M Y GRANDFATHER WAS A BRILLIANT attorney who had a photographic memory and liked to impress his clients with his ability to recall, word for word, passages from his law books that dealt with their particular cases. It is my understanding that the attorney general of the state in which my grandfather practiced law called him "one of the most brilliant attorneys he had ever met." Although my grandfather was highly intelligent in his field, he made a mess of his personal life and family.

I don't know how long my grandfather had an alcohol problem or when it started, but when he was drunk, any normalcy in the home changed. When my grandfather was sober, all was well, and money was no problem.

When he was on one of his drinking binges, however, he would go on a spending spree, as my father called it, hire a driver and limousine, and take off for New York or Florida. It was not uncommon for him to be away for several weeks or even several months, leaving behind little food for the family to survive and no money to purchase groceries.

One time, Dad, his sister, and his mother ate nothing but biscuits with gravy, made from fatback bacon, which was almost pure fat. Another time, for two months, dried apples, peaches, and biscuits were all they ate for their three daily meals. Added to their misery was the fact that the home was never a constant in their lives—fourteen times the family moved because Grandfather spent the money on hard liquor before the rent was paid.

Squandering money on alcohol was not the only problem the family faced. When my grandfather was drinking heavily, he became mean. Stephen Foster songs became a dread, and Dad hated them, even into his elder years. Yanked out of bed at two or three o'clock in the morning, my dad and aunt, only very young children at the time, were made to stand and join Grandfather in Foster songs as he slurred out the words from his intoxicated breath. On other occasions, Dad was awakened and marched out into the night air, where he was put in Grandfather's car and driven nine to ten miles down a country road. There, he was put out of the car and left alone by the side of a road, as the car drove away. How frightened Dad must have felt as he walked the dark country road, trying to find his way back home.

On more than one occasion, as a young boy, Dad went to his mother's aid as she tried to wrestle a gun from his father's hands before he accidentally shot both of them. Surprisingly, Grandmother never sought help for herself or her children. Domestic abuse was not a topic talked about in her day. Besides, she felt it her duty to pretend that everything was fine and to cover for her husband, for fear of damaging his law career. Much later in life, when she was a widow, whenever I tried to ask her about it, she would turn the subject to something else and deny that anything had ever been wrong. What I did not understand then, I understand now.

As Dad grew older, he took jobs delivering papers and clothing to customers around his neighborhood. The small amount of money he made helped to purchase a few groceries for the family when his father was gone. And as always, Grandmother pretended that everything was going well, smiling as she went to church and various social events.

By the time Dad was ten years old, he had developed an intense desire to become a champion prizefighter. He loved watching episodes of Kid Roberts in *Leather Pushers* at the local theater and fantasized that life as a boxer to be very glamorous. Hanging a punching bag in the shed behind his house, he punched it relentlessly every day in his resolve to fight in the ring someday.

Dad was a small boy in stature, but at night, under the street lights in front of one of the grocery stores, Dad boxed any boy who would fight in the neighborhood. He would size up any new boy who moved into the neighborhood and decide how that boy would be vulnerable in a fight. With the family constantly moving, there were always new boys to fight, and he was happy to oblige them.

When he wasn't dreaming of becoming a champion prizefighter, he turned to his second love, the guitar. Since his parents didn't care for the guitar, wanting instead for him to play either the piano or violin, he was forbidden to bring his beloved instrument inside to practice. Undaunted and with more determination, he would go into the woods with the ninety-eight–cent secondhand guitar he had purchased and practice the lessons taught by an accomplished guitar teacher, whom he had found in that area. For hours on end in the summers, he enjoyed the warmth of the woods as he practiced, and in the cold of winter, he would return to the woods, build a fire, and continue practicing. It was this determination to become a good musician, coupled with a gifted talent that benefited him throughout his lifetime.

As he grew older, he was rewarded for his outstanding academics by promotion to a higher grade; in fact, he skipped grades two times. By the time he was sixteen, Dad had graduated from high school with straight As. With twenty-five hard-earned dollars in his pocket and old enough to do so, he left home and headed off to college in the fall. By this time, his father's health was deteriorating from the many years of alcoholism, and any monies his parents might have saved were going for doctor bills. Dad was totally focused on the plans he had for his life, so he worked long hours to help finance his tuition, books, room, and living expenses, while he continued to take guitar lessons, punch the bag in the college gym, and dream of becoming a champion prizefighter.

In the spring of the academic school year, bedbugs infested the dorm rooms, especially in the dorm where Dad was staying. While other young men seemed not to be bothered, Dad spent one sleepless night after another, trying to keep from being bitten; the bugs were relentless. Although he complained to the dean, it seemed that the college officials did little to stop the invasion of these biting insects. Finally, all the years of pent-up anger and frustration spilled over. In a total rage, Dad opened the window of his second-floor dorm room, picked up the furniture, tossed it out the window, and watched it slam onto the campus lawn.

This time, however, instead of the principal's office, he visited the president's office. Although the college didn't punish him because of the fear of bad publicity, he had experienced all he wanted of college life and walked away from his academics. An angry young man, he packed up his meager belongings and hitchhiked to Miami, Florida, to pursue his dream of becoming a champion fighter. There would be other times when this seething anger would rise to an explosive level.

Those early childhood experiences left an intense mark that followed him throughout his entire life. His nerves were so bad, to the point that he developed insomnia, a sleep disorder that lasted throughout his lifetime. When my brother and I were children, we would see him up at night, studying for several hours because he couldn't sleep. Girl slumber parties were rare in our home, because once Dad was awakened, he was up for the rest of the night. The crash of a pan accidentally dropped on the kitchen floor would cause him to scream. Sudden, loud noises unnerved him terribly. As he did so often as a child, Dad continued to bite his nails down to the quick, a dead giveaway of his nervousness. Trying to quit seemed futile; fortunately, he did manage to break the habit in his later years

2

The Cornfield Haymaker

AFTER DAYS OF HITCHHIKING, DAD arrived in Miami, Florida, where he found a huge gymnasium that served as the workout gym for a large number of boxers, some well-known but many, like Dad, hoping for that one break to show their fighting skills.

Among the notables were Sammy Mandel, lightweight champion of the world; Mickey Walker, middleweight champion of the world; and Jimmy Maloney. There, Dad met Bill Gore, who was considered one of the best trainers of that time and who managed Willie Pep in his bid several years later to become the featherweight champion of the world.

Here was Dad, a seventeen-year-old, possibly a little cocky, and so anxious to start that he knocked on Bill Gore's door, walked in, and enthusiastically announced, "I'm Johnny Rhame, and I'm a fighter!" Smiling, Bill Gore said, "You are? Give me the names of some of the fighters you have fought." Dad mentioned the names of several of the boys back in his hometown whom he had boxed; of course, the man had never heard of them. It didn't take Gore long to perceive that Dad knew nothing about professional boxing. However, when he saw that Dad weighed around 122 pounds and was in excellent shape, Mr. Gore asked if Dad would like to step into one of the rings and box a couple of rounds. He needed a fighter Dad's size to fill in for a boxer who was unable to fight in an opener that was coming up in a couple of days.

He took Dad into the gym, where fighters were jumping rope, sparring with their partners in the ring, shadow boxing, and punching light and heavy bags. Gore asked him, "Do you want to fight?"

"Yes, sir," Dad replied.

"See those fighters?" Gore asked. "Which one do you want to fight?"

"It doesn't matter to me," Dad said. "I'll take on any of them."

The fight card that Gore thought Dad could possibly fill was not an important fight; it was a curtain-raiser, better known as a four-round preliminary. He simply wanted to see if Dad could actually fight and to size up his physical shape. After motioning for one of the fighters to come over and box with Dad for a few minutes, Gore gave the fighter instructions not to hit very hard. Without knowing that these instructions had been given to his opponent, when the sixteen-ounce gloves were placed on Dad's hands, he went out and gave it all he had for about three minutes, and then time was called.

To Dad's advantage, it was enough time for Gore to see that Dad could handle being in the ring. He asked if Dad would like to fight in the curtain-raiser at the Coliseum in Coral Gables on that Thursday evening. Amazingly, Dad had never seen a professional boxing match but was so excited about being asked that he agreed to box in the opening match.

Thursday night arrived. Since this was the curtain-raiser, he went into the match without a clue as to what to expect or how he should conduct himself in the ring. The gymnasium manager, suspecting that Dad knew very little about boxing, advised him to do exactly what his second told him to do—a second is the man in the corner who advises the fighter tactically, gives him a pep talk, and attends to his wounds throughout the fight.

The referee called Dad and his opponent to the center of the ring to give instructions. Too nervous to comprehend what was being said, Dad went back to his corner totally dismayed and not really knowing what to expect. Billy Kelly, an up-and-coming young welterweight in his own ranks and Dad's second for the fight, told him to keep his hands up high and go out there and fight his best. He intended that Dad should keep his hands a little above his shoulders, but Dad did not know what that meant. Seasoned fighters know that a boxer dropping his hands to his sides and not keeping his hands up is one of the biggest mistakes that can be made in the ring. The good news was that Dad followed Kelly's instructions—he held up his hands. The bad news was that he held his hands so high he left himself exposed. Excited, nervous, and confused as what to do next, he just kept dancing around with his hands held high.

You can only imagine what took place in that ring. Dad took quite a beating in the first round without landing a single blow on his opponent. By the time he went to his corner to wait for the second bell, the skin was peeled off his nose, his lips and face had begun swelling, and blood poured from his ears. The seconds started talking to one another, "This fighter doesn't know what to do when you tell him what to do. There's no use. He'll never make it through four rounds." While they were cleaning him up, they told him to just go back out, fight his best, and remember to keep his hands up. It's still a mystery to me why they never changed his strategy or explained to him what he was doing wrong.

The second round began, and, once again, Dad did as he had been instructed. He started dancing around with his hands held high, leaving him exposed again. What happened next is something we might expect to see today on a sports channel replay for an unbelievable fight. Totally bewildered, Dad's opponent stopped dead in his tracks, dropped his hands to his side, stuck out his chin, and spit right in Dad's face. Later in life, when Dad retold this story, he said, "I didn't know the right way to hit, but I sure knew the wrong way." In a flash and totally enraged by the insult, he swung into action and hit his opponent in the chin with, as it was called in his hometown in Carolina, "a cornfield haymaker."

The tremendous side blow caught the fighter by surprise, and he staggered and sat down hard on the floor of the ring. Not having a clear knowledge of the rules and being so infuriated, Dad swung the other gloved fist and straightened him out. The referee yelled, "You can't do that!"

Dad yelled back, "Oh yes, I can!" and hit him again. By now, the wounded fighter's legs were on the inside and his body on the outside of the ropes. In a flash, Dad reached outside of the ring, grabbed the dazed fighter by the hair, and began to punch him in the face.

When the referee ran over to stop the fight, Dad turned and punched the referee in the face, knocking him out as well. By this time, his opponent's handlers and Dad's seconds, along with the police, were scrambling into the ring to stop the fight. When it finally was stopped, Dad was told that he was disqualified, yet even so, the fight promoter paid him. To Dad's way of thinking, having that paycheck in his pocket meant that he really had *not* been disqualified.

The next day, a full-page article appeared in the sports section of the newspaper that read, "Young Lightweight Comes Out of the Hills of Carolina, Broke Every Rule in the Ring, Made Some More, and Broke Them." It was possibly the best publicity a beginning fighter could have received, but Dad didn't know it. He was so green. Instead, he was terribly insulted by all the publicity the fight had generated.

To his utter dismay when he arrived at the gym for his workout the next morning, a huge throng of admirers were waiting for him. Too young and inexperienced to understand the importance of the paper's publicity, he was embarrassed. Even so, the crowd had loved the unorthodox medley, and the beginning of his fighting career had been launched.

3

That's Quite a Thing

T HE FOLLOWING DAY, DETERMINED TO learn this sport, Dad contacted a boxing manager. Day after day this man taught Dad the fundamentals of boxing. At the same time as he was gaining knowledge about fighting and having two scheduled fights a month, he continued to practice his guitar religiously.

One day, he decided to go down to WIOD, one of the largest Miami radio stations in southern Florida, and asked, "Would you like to have someone play and sing for you on the station?" It was the same forward innocence that he had used when telling Gore his name and that he was a fighter. Interested in hearing Dad play, the radio station arranged an audition, where he played and sang a couple of numbers. As soon as he had finished auditioning, the station gave him a fifteen-minute slot as a guest artist for one of their programs. To Dad's delight, another field was opening up, and he was off and running.

It just so happened one day that the fight promoter heard him play and sing on the radio. Impressed by what he was hearing, he arranged to have a radio set up in the gymnasium and turned up loudly enough so all the fighters could hear Dad play. This addition became a regular part of their routine as they worked out. The promoter also told Dad that if he could arrange to also announce the upcoming fights, not only could he have all the fights he wanted, but the promoter would fix it so Dad would not get hurt.

That was huge to Dad because in the winter months, around fifteen hundred boxers came to Miami, and fights were hard to get. If a fighter had one good match over a certain period, he was doing well. Dad agreed, and it was arranged that he would announce the upcoming fights in exchange for getting everyone at the station all the fight tickets they wanted.

The promoter did just what he promised, but after about twenty-five fights, Dad was tired of the pushovers, the new and inexperienced fighters, and the fighters who were already punch-drunk. He really wanted to fight, so he decided to leave Miami and go to Jacksonville, Florida, where he introduced himself to Leo Cavanaugh, another manager and trainer in the boxing world. When Cavanaugh saw Dad walk in, he started laughing. He had been at his first fight and remembered who he was, and he joked about what a fight that had been.

Cavanaugh had a large home with a stable of fighters who lived there. Dad was invited to join the group; so he began this new residence with these same fighters with whom he routinely did his road work of running ten miles every morning before breakfast and then returning to work out. Now, he started getting what he considered legitimate fights, for which he really had to know what he was doing. In addition to working out and fighting, he continued practicing his guitar for several hours a day.

As Dad was practicing one day, one of the fighters was so impressed with Dad's musical abilities that he told him he should take his guitar down to their gym to play. After hearing Dad play and sing, Ed Corely, the fight promoter, told him, "That's quite a thing—a fighter playing a guitar. I want you to do that. Take your guitar down to the ring, and play it for the crowd."

When the night came for the scheduled fight, Dad took his guitar ringside, where a crowd of several thousand had gathered to see the event of the evening. Although he wasn't fighting in that match, it was announced that one of their fighters, who was also an accomplished guitarist, would be playing and singing before the fight.

When he finished performing before the enthusiastic crowd, a talent scout and an agent, who had been in the stands, came over to meet him. They talked to him about quitting the ring and launching into entertaining, saying he would make more money playing in nightclubs than fighting in the ring. "Besides," the talent scout said, "it would be a lot easier on the nose." That may have rung a bell because by that time, Dad had lost a lot of the cartilage in his nose. Dad's interest was piqued. The agent set about arranging an engagement for him in a one of the clubs.

For some reason, playing before a nightclub audience made him more nervous than playing before a crowded boxing match. When the evening came for him to perform, about an hour before he was to go on stage, he went to the manager and said, "I can't play."

"Of course you can play!" the manager replied,

"I can't remember the words to the song," Dad insisted, "and not even the chords to the guitar. I am so nervous that I can't do this."

"Come with me," the manager said. He took Dad inside his office and poured a glass of whiskey, with the promise that Dad's nerves would calm down in about fifteen minutes. "If this doesn't calm you enough," the manager told him, "I'll pour you another glass."

By the time Dad went out to perform, his nerves were steady, and his show was a tremendous success. The very thing Dad had despised all the years growing up by "taking a drink" was the very thing that he embraced and credited with helping him get through the performance that night. From that time on, he would not play and sing unless he had several drinks. Sadly, drinking became more and more a part of his life.

Ironically, during the last part of his boxing career, he was entertaining on the side, as opposed to the first part of his entertainment career, where his main focus had been on boxing. Even with drinking before each show, he managed to stay in excellent physical shape. By 1932, he was tired of boxing and all the rules required by the physical trainers. Besides, he was doing well financially as a professional entertainer. The fact that Dad had seen a close friend become punch-drunk from too many fights helped him make the decision to quit before this ever happened to him.

He went on to book his last fight with Jimmy Crowder, who was defending his title as the lightweight champion of Tennessee. It was a great test of boxing skills, as each fought with all his strength. At the end of the fight, the judges' decisions were in favor of the champion, and Dad lost the fight. The crowd booed the decision, and Dad was encouraged to challenge the outcome. Knowing that he was quitting the ring, he simply lacked the interest to pursue the challenge and decided to let it drop. So after fifty-six fights, with a record of thirty-six by knockouts, eleven decisions, six draws, three losses, and the rest wins, he left the ring and threw himself into the world of entertainment, traveling from one club to another, playing all over the country. Soon, he began acquiring a national reputation as a musical artist and comedian. Although he was experiencing success with his new career, anger issues continued to plague him.

One day while driving down a city street in southern Florida, he ran a red light. He had just come from a nightclub where he had been performing and drinking a little too much. As he drove through the light, a policeman yelled at him, ordering him to stop. Dad stepped out of his car, reached down to pick up his steel guitar, and walked back to where two officers now stood. When they asked him why he had run the red light, he began playing and singing "I'll Be Glad When You're Dead, You Rascal, You." As the police started to arrest him, a fight ensued, and Dad hit one of the officers over the head with his guitar. Then, seeing the other officer coming toward him,

Dad threw his guitar at him. Fortunately, it missed, but the damage was done. Dad was arrested and placed in jail for several days. They finally released him on the condition that he would never return to that city.

At other times, Dad's deep anger spilled over in unimaginable ways. On one occasion, while driving to keep a nightclub engagement, his car suddenly stopped running. He tried one thing and then another to get it started, but not having any mechanical ability, it was futile. Infuriated and blinded by rage, he retrieved a sledge hammer from the trunk of his car and totally demolished the vehicle, smashing out the windows and then the headlights and beating in its sides and roof. Although he was completely exhausted, he knew he had to arrive at his engagement on time, so he hitchhiked to a car dealership, paid cash for a new car, and drove away, having left the battered car by the side of the road several miles back.

While playing at two theaters in Gladewater, Texas, he decided to make it a night of drinking and partying. After he arrived at his hotel room at three o'clock in the morning, he heard cars screech to a stop outside his window. Looking out, he saw several men and women pouring out of their automobiles and quarreling. In a short time, a fight began. Still inebriated, Dad listened to all of the commotion outside and then angrily reached into his suitcase and brought out his boxing gloves and the trunks that he always kept with him from his fighting days. Putting them on, he staggered downstairs, walked into the street, and began to fight one person and then another. When he heard the wail of the police sirens, he simply turned around, walked back up into his room, and went to bed as if nothing had happened. Fear was never a part of his DNA. He simply wanted a good night's rest, and, to his way of thinking, the fight outside wasn't going to prevent this from happening.

While entertaining in a roadhouse in Nebraska, Dad found himself in a situation that almost cost him his life. As he was playing and singing, two gangs walked into the bar. After several drinks, something happened that triggered an angry exchange between the two groups, and a fight broke out. In a flash, both sides pulled out guns and began shooting at one another. With the realization that his life was in danger, Dad jumped off the stage, with his steel guitar in front of him for protection, and dove for cover under a table, while bullets flew across the room. That guitar was the only thing that saved his life. To this day, the refurbished dents, now barely seen, are still in that old guitar, which I have in my possession.

Dad's past as a fighter also continued to follow him. He had been known for his lightning-fast hands. One of his stops landed him with several engagements at a nightclub owned by a former professional wrestler. Numerous times—and while intoxicated—the owner would want to see if Dad's fists were better than his own wrestling moves. No matter how much Dad tried to avoid getting into a confrontation, the owner finally cornered Dad and forced the issue. Dad's fists were too much for the man, and he pummeled him into submission. The owner said the incident would not affect Dad's position as an entertainer in his club, but Dad knew the time would come when he would have to prove himself again, and rather than risk being fired, he decided to move on.

There are other stories—stories of how he survived other life-threatening situations while playing in nightclubs or unknowingly hanging out with men of questionable character. How he survived some of those situations, I shall never know. He shared several that I failed to write down or record, and although I know parts of them, I fear I will not tell them accurately; others, he chose not to disclose. I realized that some may have been too painful to talk about, so I did not push him to reveal those portions of his life. Thankfully, Dad's story does not end here, for had he continued on the path he was choosing, I doubt if he would have lived many more years, and his story would have had little significance to inspire others.

4

Lunch Brought Much More than Just a Sandwich

IT WAS CUSTOMARY FOR DAD to remain in a place for two or three days before moving to his next engagement. If he wasn't entertaining in one of the night spots, he was out partying. Soon, it began to bother him that the physical shape of which he had been so proud when he was training for a fight was now deteriorating. He was smoking two to three packs of cigarettes a day, as well as drinking a pint to a quart of whiskey each day. Several times, he tried to quit, but the addictions had become so strong that he would fail in any attempts to withdraw. Besides, he felt drinking the whiskey made him perform better. Finally, he reached the point that he did not care anymore.

By then, he had gained a measure of popularity and enough money to purchase anything he wanted. He loved entertaining and playing his guitar; he was quite a showman. Often, he would toss out a spinning chair, and, to the enjoyment of the crowd, he would sit down on the seat and play his guitar, just as it stopped twirling. Even though he did not have long slender fingers, they would fly effortlessly from one end of the guitar neck to the other end, to the applause of the audience. He could play and sing just about anything that was requested, knowing well over four hundred songs from memory. Being funny only added to his showmanship. With Dad's quick wit and the ability to recall jokes and make up new ones, men would literally fall out of their chairs from laughter. Yet even while experiencing this success, he did not find the inward happiness for which he had been searching since he left his home at sixteen

It was 1933 in the small town of Gladewater, Texas; Dad had an engagement at the Payne Theater. The advertisement for his show was posted all over Gladewater and surrounding towns. Often, he would eat lunch at one of the local restaurants because he rarely ate dinner before his performance.

One woman in Gladewater not only owned a fine restaurant, but she also would often wait on those tables.

A couple of days after Dad arrived for his engagement, he made his way to her restaurant. When he walked in, she recognized him from the pictures around town, plus she had heard about this new entertainer.

After he ordered a meal and was waiting for his food, she introduced herself and struck up a conversation. About that time, Rev. E. T. Harris, the pastor of the Nazarene church where she was a member, walked in. After greeting him, she asked if he would like to meet the new entertainer who was performing at the Payne Theater that night.

"I'd love to meet him," the pastor said, and she introduced the two men. With a big smile on his face, Reverend Harris asked Dad if he could join him for lunch. Dad was glad for the company.

As they got acquainted, Dad learned that Reverend Harris also loved music and played the guitar, and the two talked about music and show business. Impressive features about Reverend Harris were his huge smile and his friendly demeanor; he made Dad feel very comfortable while they talked. How insightful that this pastor never mentioned anything pertaining to a man's spiritual condition. His goal for that moment was to form a relationship with Dad.

After they finished eating and visiting and were on their way out the door, this godly and very wise pastor invited Dad to drive over with him to the radio station, where the pastor would soon go on the air for a religious broadcast. Out of curiosity, Dad consented to go. On the way to the station, Reverend Harris invited Dad to attend his church, where revival services were being held. Not only did he invite Dad to attend, but he shared with Dad how much his congregation liked guitar playing, and he extended an invitation to play. The Nazarene denomination was very conservative in its earlier days, and the guitar was often frowned upon for playing in worship. Generally the organ and piano were the instruments of choice. I am still amazed by this man's intuitiveness. His inviting a nightclub and theater entertainer—someone he had just met—to come to his church to play and sing was his way of extending love and grace to a man who had no idea what any of it meant.

Not knowing what he was getting himself into, Dad agreed to play for the congregation on one of the nights when he wasn't performing; it would be the first time he thought about entering a church since he was sixteen years old. He had no knowledge of any religious music, so one can only imagine what he played. When I asked him, he couldn't remember the song he used but merely said, with a twinkle in his eye, "I just played and sang."

As Dad walked into the church for the first time, he saw a man kneeling and praying at an altar. He whispered to someone nearby, "What is wrong with that man?" The person told him that the man was praying "through," a church term used when someone is seeking the Lord's forgiveness of sins. Dad, new to the religious jargon, replied, "Praying through what?"

While Dad continued performing in Gladewater and at other theaters and clubs throughout the surrounding areas at night, he also started broadcasting for a music store during the daytime. As the days went by, a mutual friendship grew between Dad and the pastor. What was to have been a normal one- or two-week revival stretched out over nine weeks, as Reverend Harris and his congregation hoped to have an impact on Dad's life, using first one speaker and then another. For nine weeks, on the few nights he was able to attend, Dad was drawn by the sweet spirit demonstrated in the music and in the warmth and acceptance of the people who made up the congregation.

When he was growing up, church held no real meaning for him, although he memorized the entire catechism of his family's church. Church was merely the social gathering for his parents and the prestigious place to worship in the community. Dad, however, was turned off by the church soloist, who would be out drinking and getting drunk on Saturday night, only to show up and pretend to be spiritual while he sang on Sunday morning. Dad felt the man was no different from his dad and vowed never to be a part of any church when he was old enough to make that decision. In Reverend Harris's church, though, something was different. The people's faith and genuineness did not hold the hypocrisy of the church in which he had grown up.

For the first time, he heard the message of the love of God and His grace, how Jesus had died on the cross to forgive men of their sins, how His love would cover all the things Dad had done in his life that were wrong, how the Lord had a purpose for his life that included peace and a fresh renewing of his life, and how he could have a personal relationship with the heavenly Father.

Dad was touched, not only by the message but by the kindness and love that was poured out on him by the members of this church. When different members would pick him up to go to church, no one asked him to change or tried to preach to him. Dad was a chain-smoker, but even with the car windows rolled up against the cold January air, and Dad's lighting up one cigarette after another as they drove to church, there wasn't a word of criticism. I am sure they all smelled like smoke when they walked into the service. Over the ensuing weeks, while he was going about his business of performing and broadcasting, every family in the church extended an invitation for him to come to their homes for a home-cooked meal. Dad had never known such hospitality and warmth as they continued to show their love.

On January 17, 1933, Dad made the decision that he would once again attend the evening service, but this time, it would be to ask forgiveness and give his life to the Lord. For several days, his heart had been feeling drawn to the message of the saving grace of Christ Jesus. Now, he was ready to commit.

During the evening's message, he thought, *Will this speaker ever stop preaching?* When the service finally came to an end, Dad walked to the front of the church to make this life-changing decision. He knelt at an altar of prayer and asked God to forgive him of his sins. An inner peace, unlike any he had ever experienced, washed over him, and he felt completely free for the first time in his life. The pastor and everyone in the church were ecstatic. Rather than being just a building where the gospel was preached, it was now a rescue mission for a young man who had been on a path to destruction.

Dad was so excited that he could hardly wait to tell his buddies, who were entertaining in nearby clubs and theaters, about the love and grace of Christ Jesus and the new faith he now embraced. He didn't have a clue as to how to go about sharing the gospel to them, so when he saw any of his friends walking down the street, he simply grabbed each by the shirt and said, "You have to be saved!" It wasn't long before his friends would turn around and run away when they saw him coming. As unbelievers, they could not comprehend the transformation that had taken place in Dad's life. Religion did not spring to mind when they saw him. I imagine some of them thought he had lost his mind.

This life-changing experience left Dad on a high for only so long. Unfortunately, all the destructive habits against a healthy lifestyle were still there and had taken their toll. To live the existence that he had lived for so many years was not easily erased. Change takes discipline, time, and, sometimes, a special anointing of the Holy Spirit. I have personally heard stories of new believers who have wrestled with addictive behaviors, where there is no longer a desire for those behaviors. Recovery is instant, and they are completely free. However, this was not the case for Dad. He began to shake, and at night he would toss and turn while sleep eluded him. This went on for days. Finally, in frustration, he slipped out of bed and walked as far as ten miles down the railroad tracks, trying to calm his nerves, before coming back to lie awake again. After six weeks, he had a nervous breakdown, and a doctor came to see him.

When the doctor examined him, he asked, "What have you been doing to yourself?" When Dad told him of the spiritual transformation that had come into his life and his desire to live without the addictions that had been destroying his health and life, the doctor explained, "That is the trouble. You must not go cold turkey. Go back and use some tobacco again and a little whiskey, or you will go insane."

After the doctor left, Dad lay on his bed, thinking over what the doctor had said. As thoughts of the past raced through his mind, he resolved, in that instant, that he would rather die than go back to his old lifestyle of the past several years—a lifestyle that had not brought the happiness he had been seeking.

Dad didn't know enough about Scriptures or the promises of God to recite them for strength, but immediately, as he cried out to the Lord and verbally proclaimed his desire to walk with Him, no matter the cost, even if it meant death, he could feel a healing touch. It started at the top of his head and went down to the bottom of his feet. It was an amazing experience, and, in that instant, all the cravings were gone—completely vanished. God had heard his cry. For Johnny Rhame—prizefighter, musical artist, and comedian—God did have a purpose and a plan for his life that would take him completely in another direction, if he would follow God, and follow Him, he did.

Becoming a Christ-follower, however, may not instantaneously take care of leftover troubled issues that can plaque a person. Damaged emotions from memories, actions, and past behaviors in one's life need time to repair and reprogram. For Dad, one of the issues with which he continued to struggle was anger, especially from his childhood.

One Sunday, Reverend Harris preached on the power of the Holy Spirit in the lives of believers with regard to guiding and directing them through their Christian walk. Becoming a born-again Christian, he said, was the beginning of a changed life, but it also was something more. It was seeking guidance from the Holy Spirit over a lifetime, in all areas of one's life, including life issues that needed a special touch and having a relationship with the Lord and others. Dad listened intently but scoffed at the idea that he needed to have a closer walk with the Lord through the power of the Holy Spirit. "Why?" he asked. "I have everything I need in this new life. That is probably meant for someone else."

It wasn't long before an incident occurred that made him realize he still had a lot of pent-up anger. He was walking down the street, and just as he approached a driveway, the man of the house came running out, jumped into his car, and, without looking behind him, started backing out—just as Dad was walking past. As he jumped to avoid being hit, the car passed so close that it brushed his clothes. In a flash, Dad angrily yelled at the driver to stop. Before the driver realized what was taking place, Dad ran over, grabbed the man by the collar, drew back his fist, and said, "You big stiff! You might have killed me. I am going to knock your head off!"

Just then, he had a moment of realization—walking with and serving the Lord did not include beating up people, as he would have done in the past. He turned the man loose, apologized, and returned to his room, where he knelt beside his bed and asked God to forgive him and purge him of any unrighteous anger. If this meant having the Holy Spirit as a part of his life, he wanted everything God had to offer. Again, his prayers were answered, and from that time onward, Dad's days of wanting to fight were over. He still had a quick temper, but now, the difference was in the way the Holy Spirit guided him in dealing with this issue. The refinement had started.

5

He Left the Stage to Preach the Gospel

In the same way he eagerly learned how to fight and became an accomplished guitarist, Dad embraced his newfound faith—faith that did not come without tremendous sacrifices. He chose some of the sacrifices, while others were made for him without any choice on his part. His conversion took place in the worst times of the Great Depression.

He decided to leave behind a world he had known for several years and embarked on new ways to earn a living. Having no real life skills, however, and only having attended college for a few months, he found it difficult to get employment that could afford him the income to which he had become accustomed. When he applied for a job and was asked about his past employment, he didn't know whether he should say he had been a professional boxer or musical entertainer. Regardless of which choice he gave, he couldn't find work.

With sadness, he left Gladewater and traveled to Hot Springs, Arkansas, where, quite by accident, he met a man on the street who was a member of the First Church of the Nazarene in that city. Dad was invited to attend the worship service on Sunday, where he met the pastor and his wife. After Dad shared his story and his inability to find work, the pastor called all the members together and explained Dad's situation.

One of the members, Harvey Pool, offered Dad a job— peddling eggs. Dad thought, *When I asked the Lord for a job, I never said anything about peddling eggs*, but he asked, "How do you peddle eggs?"

"Just take a hamper basket in either hand," Harvey explained, "and go from house to house."

Carrying eggs in a basket from house to house was not the kind of job Dad had hoped to find. As he began to think of excuses why he couldn't do this, a verse of Scripture that he had recently studied in Matthew 25:21, reminded him that if he was good and faithful over a few things, even with eggs, that God would make him ruler over many (KJV). He decided he would give it a try.

The job paid a living at first; eggs sold for thirty cents a dozen. Then the price started falling, and eggs went down to eight or nine cents a dozen. In time, he started looking for another job. Here was a man who had been making between two hundred and four hundred dollars a night (big money for that time), who was now selling eggs and barely making a substandard living. Before long, he had to sell his car.

Discouraged when he couldn't find anything, he decided to hitchhike his way to his parents' home in South Carolina. Travel was not as easy as it had been in the past. With no money and only a few clothes and his guitar, he took one job after another as he hitchhiked and walked for several weeks from one town to the next and painted houses.

Finally arriving home, he shared with his parents his faith conversion, his departure from boxing, and his diminished need for fame and fortune in the world of nightclubs and roadhouses. What he had hoped would be a happy reunion was met with anger as his father cursed and told him what a stupid thing he had done. During the time Dad had made money in the ring or in entertaining, he had sent his parents a sizable amount of money to help pay for his father's medical bills. With the realization that this money would no longer be available, his father was angry.

"You've been given the talent to make a lot of money," he stormed at Dad, "and now you've thrown it all away!"

Feeling unwanted and knowing that he could not stay at home—there was no work for him, and his invalid father and mother had very little money left—he once again began making his way across the country. Winter had set in, and he ate where he could find food and slept nights in the woods or beside the road. Often, he walked with hair matted from the freshly fallen snow. It was a terrible transition to be homeless, lonely, cold, and hungry as he journeyed for several weeks from one town to the next.

Never without his guitar, he fortunately found several churches that welcomed him and, upon hearing his story, invited him to sing and play his guitar during one of their services. In these churches were godly and caring men who befriended him and gave him a place to eat and sleep. Soon, several evangelists heard about Dad, his conversion, and his musical abilities, and they invited him to join them in singing and playing in their meetings. Dad had never heard of such a thing as evangelistic work, but his interest was piqued once again.

It was during this time he met C. M. Whitely and his wife, evangelists in the Church of the Nazarene, who had several meetings scheduled throughout the area. They invited Dad to travel with them and sing in their meetings, so for seven weeks, Dad found comfort and a place to use his musical talents. This time, however, it was not just a show but a place in which he could serve others.

By the end of the seven weeks, Dad received a call from Mississippi's district superintendent, an official who oversees all the churches in that state, to come and help him in a scheduled meeting with one of the church's general superintendents, Dr. John Goodman. Dr. Goodman held the distinct honor of being one of several men at the head of the entire denomination. To Dad's credit—and the affirming praise from the congregations—he did all the special music for four weeks while Dr. Goodman preached.

Night after night, he listened to the wisdom of God's Word, and during the day, he spent quality time with Dr. Goodman and his wife. Dad shared with the Goodmans that he felt the call to preach—a call he did not take lightly. Instead of telling Dad that he was too green or that his past life would be a hindrance, Dr. Goodman invited him to the home where he was staying, and every afternoon, he taught and mentored Dad, not in the ways of the denomination but in God's Word. Dad was very appreciative because throughout his life, he had searched out successful men who were knowledgeable in their field. Now, he was eager to learn from successful men in the church—a learning trait he would carry for the rest of his life.

It was during these study session that Dad began to understand more completely the biblical truths that were presented to him. Dad believed that God had sent this couple into his life at a time when he needed them the most—the many months following his conversion had been such difficult ones as he struggled with different issues. In November 1934, Johnny Rhame, former prizefighter, musician, and comedian, held his first revival, and a ministry was launched.

The following year, while Dad was holding a revival in Charlottesville, Virginia, a young entertainer named Tommy Younce, who had known Dad as a performer and friend, walked past the church where Dad was scheduled to preach that evening. On the billboard was Dad's name and the time when the preaching service would begin. Seeing the name was such a shock to Tommy that he decided to attend the service to see if this was really his old friend.

Walking into the church, Tommy was amazed to see that it was indeed the man with whom he had played and sung in nightclubs in days past. At the close of the service, Tommy walked down to the front, where Dad was greeting and praying with people. It was quite a reunion—they hadn't seen each other in a long time. Tommy asked Dad one question after another, and Dad shared the gospel of

Christ, just as he had heard and was preaching about it. Under conviction, Tommy asked Dad to pray with him, and as fate would have it, the two of them prayed together, and Tommy gave his heart to the Lord. For the next five months, they traveled together, with Dad preaching and the two of them playing and singing. I know how talented the two of them were, so I am sure they provided musical, high-energy revival services.

As God's purpose played out in their lives, Tommy confided in Dad that he also felt the call to go into full-time ministry. It was a time of celebration, knowing that the Holy Spirit indeed was guiding and directing their lives. Hence, the two departed, each going his own way, and Tommy left for Richmond, Virginia, to prepare himself for what God had ordained. It was in Richmond that Tommy would impact his brother, Bernard, who was also a guitarist and entertainer. It was not long before Bernard gave his heart to the Lord. They made quite a musical team as well. When the time was right, and they felt prepared to step out and share God's Word, both Tommy and Bernard went into the evangelistic field, eventually becoming full-time pastors. Dad had been faithful, and God was blessing.

Tommy and Bernard often called Dad to come and hold a revival for their churches. In the course of events, they would all marry and bring additional friendship, through their wives, with one another. Throughout their lifetimes, they stayed in touch, never straying from the gospel, never tiring of the message of God's forgiving love and grace. They preached it over and over, until the day arrived when age dictated that this season of their lives had come to an end. Dad's personal decision in 1933—and his tenacious commitment to a lifestyle of change in following God's course for his life—made a profound impact in the lives of these two fine and talented men.

6

A Sleuth in Love

I T WAS AUGUST 1935, AND Mother was a teenager, young and pretty, attending the annual church camp in northeast Maryland. Church camps in Maryland were always exciting times for church members and their pastors. Church members would drive from towns and cities across Pennsylvania, Maryland, and New Jersey to spend a week listening to well-traveled evangelists share their faith, while enjoying special music performed by talented musicians. It was also a week filled with seeing old friends and meeting new people from across the state.

Cabins and tents dotted the wooded area that also housed a large dining room and outdoor tabernacle, where church services were held. Three meals were prepared in the dining hall for those campers who could afford the luxury of purchasing daily meal tickets. The aroma of home cooking from the rest of the cabins wafted over the grounds each day. A huge dinner bell rang three times for meals and once for each of the three daily services— morning, afternoon, and evening. It was a safe place of comfort and fun. The camp was not a long drive from Mother's home in Port Elizabeth, New Jersey, and she and her mother had eagerly prepared for this time away from their farm chores.

Mother had already heard about the handsome, dark-haired guitar player who was going to be the musician for some of the services. Having a guest musician who was once a professional entertainer was quite a treat, especially for a young girl who had not ventured very far from her home. She would definitely take stock of him, but the son of a schoolteacher back home was really her interest.

When Dad saw Mother sitting in one of the services where he was playing, he thought she was one of the most beautiful young women he had ever seen. At the conclusion of the service, Mother's brother-in-law, who was the pastor of a church in Deep Water, New Jersey, brought her over and introduced her to the guitar player. Little did she know this would be the beginning of a most unconventional romance—and a story I love telling every time I think about my father's careful and deliberate approach to romance.

Camp came to an end, and Dad and Mother went their separate ways: Mother traveled back to her farm in New Jersey, and Dad traveled to a singing engagement in another city at a revival meeting. By October, Dad was now in full-time ministry, traveling by bus and train to play his guitar, sing, and speak in churches up and down the eastern section of the country. Uncle Leslie, the brother-in-law who had introduced the two, had scheduled Dad for an October revival. As fate would have it, my grandparents decided to drive from Port Elizabeth to Deep Water to hear Dad speak. Along for the ride was Mother. Later, Dad quipped that Deep Water, New Jersey, is where he really got into "deep water."

Since Dad had never written or even contacted Mother in any way from the time they met, Mother had no idea that Dad was even slightly interested in her—until the second weekend of the revival. Dad had no car of his own, so he went to Aunt Mary, the pastor's wife and Mother's sister, and asked if she would pick up Mom for the Saturday evening's service. Delighted to be involved in a possible romance, Aunt Mary enlisted the help of her close friend in the church, and together, they drove to get Mother. I can only imagine the conversation between the two of them, in cahoots for a possible romance, as they drove to offer Mother a ride to the church service.

An eccentric beginning, it was! Like everything he did in life, from studying music to learning the fundamentals of boxing and reading and investigating the Bible, Dad knew what he wanted and set his goal. He systematically investigated Mother's background and character. He reasoned that before his intentions were known to her and because he was now a minister, the person with whom he would fall in love had to be a woman of deep faith, convictions, and character.

She must have risen to the occasion because many years later, after the pope visited St. Louis, where my brother, his wife, and their three sons were living, my youngest nephew, Tim, a young boy at the time, told his parents that the one person more religious than the pope was his gram, who was now a widow. That was probably the highest compliment he could think to give his grandmother and one she enjoyed telling throughout the rest of her life.

As unconventional as Dad's thinking on romance was, he was sold on the idea of knowing all about her before their first date. However, being the independent woman my mother was, I wonder if things would have been different, had she known. He never told her until sometime later, and I can only imagine that he laughed mischievously the whole time he divulged his detective work. I guess it never occurred to Mother to investigate his background; then again, whoever heard of such a thing before a guy comes calling?

After another month of investigation and soul searching, Dad decided to take the risk and grab a bus to Mother's home to declare his love for her. It was on this very first night in her living room that he mustered up enough nerve to ask her to become his wife. Surprisingly, Mother gave him the answer he had hoped for, on the condition that her father was in favor of the marriage. I think it's safe to say that after they were introduced back at camp, her interest in the schoolteacher's son back home had definitely waned. It probably never occurred to Dad to ask permission of her parents first, but before Grandfather gave his permission, my very independent grandmother had a serious talk with Dad. Although she liked him, it must have been difficult for each to give permission, knowing Mother would be traveling and not living near them after she married.

Mother was the baby of the family, with five sisters and two brothers, and she definitely was a daddy's girl. Pop Pop, as we called him, worked long and hard hours, and every chance she could, Mother would ride on the wagon with her dad throughout their farmland. All they could afford were the necessities of life. The soles of Mother's shoes were made of cardboard and would come apart if it rained. Oh, how she hated it when this happened. Ever resourceful, Pop Pop would find pieces of leather, cut them out to fit, and tack them on the bottom. Growing up, Mother never owned a store-bought dress. It was a good thing that Grandmother could sew so well.

Grammy, as we all called our grandmother, was an entrepreneur, walking up and down the railroad tracks behind their home to the homes of women who needed a new dress. There, she would measure them, come home, cut out patterns, make dresses, and deliver them in order to make a little money. She also made beautiful pillows that were sold at their roadside stand, along with the vegetables and fruit they grew. Although soiled over time, I can still see the beautiful handiwork displayed in one of her pillows in my possession. Unlike my grandmother Rhame, whose spirit had suffered, Grammy was very independent.

She was a beautiful Christian, with a deep faith that she imparted to her children. When Poppop, a good man but not one to give faith much thought, would get stubborn and decide to unplug a wire or two in the car where she couldn't drive to church, she would get all of her children dressed and walk with them several miles to attend the Nazarene church in Port Elizabeth, where she was a charter member and the church's treasurer. Her faith and penchant for financial details were definitely passed on to Mom.

Watching her mother's drive caused Mom to study hard and become an over-achiever by always making good grades throughout her years in school. She also enjoyed the recognition of being the "maypole queen" at school, an honor given to the best-looking girl. Being raised on a farm may not have provided her with many of the material things of life, but she was a content young woman, a trait that would benefit her throughout her whole life.

When all was said and done, Poppop gave his blessing, and Grammy was assured that Dad would take care of their baby girl. She was only sixteen years old and ten years younger than Dad. Finally, when they were alone, Dad asked if he could pull down the window shades and, wasting no time, gave her a kiss. Later, in retelling this story that I never grew tired of hearing, she would smile and say that Dad was never one to let any grass grow under his feet.

Now there was only one more thing that Dad felt he had to do. He informed Mother that a few months earlier, he had set up a date with a woman in Maryland, where he had held a revival. The date had been made before he met Mother at camp, and he felt it his ethical duty to keep it and let this woman know of his love for Mother. Dad felt his integrity was on display, an attribute that he carried throughout his life, in and out of his ministry. Taking a bus, he traveled from New Jersey to Maryland to see the young woman. To her surprise, she found out that he had met someone else, and there would be no date and no relationship. With that, Dad left and resumed his schedule.

One might think this was a strange thing to do, especially after just having proposed to Mother, but that was Dad. He was real. He never undertook anything that affected his life or the lives of others without careful deliberation. I guess Dad wanted everything to be above reproach, and sometimes he did the craziest things to ensure his moral standards would be above criticism, even the way he fell in love. Imagine paying for a ticket to travel some distance away, just to tell a person that you are no longer interested in dating her, and you never will be. In our culture today, throwaway relationships are severed without as much as an explanation and sometimes on social media. However you want to slice what he did, it worked. Mother had captured his heart, and the way was clear for him to marry her.

By the spring of '36, Dad had saved enough money to purchase a car, and in June of that year, after holding a meeting in Clovis, New Mexico, he drove straight through to Port Elizabeth, New Jersey, stopping only briefly in South Carolina to see his parents, who had now accepted the fact that he was in ministry. His love was so great that every chance he could get, he would drive from wherever he had a meeting to see Mother, even if only for a day or two. This was no small feat as he crisscrossed the nation in towns and cities, holding revival services and trying to carry on a long-distance romance.

Their brief engagement lasted for ten months. The letters he wrote to her while he traveled showed a very romantic side of this sleuth in love. During their engagement, Dad sent money to Grammy to help with Mother's piano lessons. He saw a talent in her so impressive that he felt compelled to encourage this financially. With the lessons and an aptitude for the piano, her gift of music would become a featured part of their team. She would accompany Dad on the piano and accordion; later, he would add the Hawaiian guitar, more commonly known today as the steel guitar, which is played across the knees. Mother's rich alto voice also blended with his, just as their marriage would uniquely blend their lives together. The young girl who had never traveled very far from home was about to be launched into a career that she never imagined when she was growing up.

Mother's family did not have the money for an elaborate wedding, so she and Dad chose to be married at the same campground where they first met. It was on a Sunday evening, August 15, 1936, at the end of the year's annual camp meeting in northeast Maryland. It was a small wedding, with Uncle Leslie once again playing a key role by officiating. With very little money to go anywhere and a revival meeting right around the corner, they decided to forgo their original plans and stay on the camp grounds.

Mother went back to her mother's cabin to spend her wedding night, while Dad went back to his cabin. What a romantic way to start a marriage! In later years, when telling the story of their wedding, they would smile and exclaim, "How could one be so lucky?" My brother and I are grateful that the circumstances of their wedding night did not become a family tradition.

The next morning, they drove to my grandparents' home to spend time with family (and each other) before venturing out as a couple for their first revival meeting. I am sure Mother was nervous with anticipation in wondering what lay ahead for them. Dad was sensitive to the fact that it would be several weeks—possibly months—before Mother would have an opportunity to be home again. To his credit and love for her, no matter where they were, until the death of her parents, he saw to it that she went home regularly.

7

There's More than Water in This Well

THEIR FIRST REVIVAL MEETING TOOK them to Hollywood, Maryland. Mother would often tell people that they honeymooned in Hollywood, near California, another town not far away. The pastor at the small country church in Hollywood, Maryland, was an elderly gentleman who lived in Washington, DC, but traveled to Hollywood every weekend to minister to his small congregation. A bed and dresser had been placed in the vacant parsonage so Dad and Mom would have a place to stay. There was no such thing as making reservations in a hotel for an evangelist. Churches, especially small churches, simply could not afford to pay an evangelist to come and speak and also pay for his lodging expenses. So each day, they had to go to the home of an elderly couple, members of the church, who provided their daily meals.

Upon their arrival, Dad went down to the well behind the building to draw their drinking water. When he pulled up the first bucket, he was shocked to find a huge dead rat in the water. Totally repulsed, he took their quart thermos and drove six miles to town each day to fill it with fresh drinking water. What a sober beginning for newlyweds!

I believe God never wavered in His promise to be faithful to them if they would remain faithful to Him. They leaned upon the Scripture in Matthew 17:20, where Jesus said, "If ye have faith as small as a mustard seed, ye will say to this mountain, 'Remove hence to yonder place;' and it shall remove; and nothing shall be impossible for you'" (KJV). The rat in the water didn't move; however, what they saw was that the hearts of men were moved, as evidenced at the conclusion of their first service. Young men, who had been standing outside the small church, listening to the songs and message, were so moved by the gospel presentation that told of God's love and forgiveness of sins that they unabashedly climbed through the open windows in order to kneel at an altar of prayer. Dad and Mother's marriage may have started off meagerly by the world's standard, but they were met with God's outpouring of an abundant blessing as they watched their lives together used in a special way that night.

Their second meeting took them from that small country church to Onego, West Virginia, and five hundred people in attendance on their first night in revival. Dad had been used to large crowds when he was a prizefighter and entertainer, but this was new to Mother. She was sixteen and had only been gone two weeks from the comforts of home. I am sure she had to muster the courage just to walk up on the platform to play and sing before this large audience. I don't know how she did it.

Without question, she was suddenly catapulted into the limelight. In time, she would grow more comfortable with this new role, although her preference was always to remain in the background. From those experiences of performing and being on the platform, however, Mother acquired a grace and wisdom that made her appear much older than her teenage years.

Often, older women would seek her out for counseling, which amazed her. Over the years, until she had a stroke in her elder years that left her without the ability to talk, she was a mentor to women of all ages, especially young women who needed encouragement.

Thus, marriage to Dad set them off on a traveled adventure—an adventure that my generation knows little about, and my children's generation would find it hard to expose themselves to the kinds of sacrifice Mother and Dad encountered. It was an age when an evangelist's pay was not always very much, but if money was a factor in their service to the Lord, it was never evidenced in the postcards and letters written to their families. They were uplifting letters, telling of their travels and the results of their ministry, although I believe money can certainly lift a man's spirit, especially in the ministry. They were in love—with the message of the plan of salvation through Christ Jesus, with one another, and with seeing how God's plan shaped the events of their lives.

They traveled thousands of miles throughout the nation, singing and sharing the gospel of their faith in 193 churches, often being asked to return to the same church for future meetings. My arrival on the scene in 1941 did not slow them, but it did slow Mother's records of meetings and travel.

Mother was absolutely amazing in packing their car with Dad's instruments, her accordion, luggage with all their belongings, a portable washing machine, my crib, and all the necessities a baby needs. The only item tied to the outside of the car was my little red rocker. As a grown woman, if I wanted to know how to pack a car for a vacation, I looked to my mother. She had a penchant for packing everything one needed to travel, and I marveled at her ability to get everything in a trunk. When I asked her how she did it, she would shake her head; it still surprised her that she had been able to pack all she did.

I loved to hear the stories they shared of staying in different homes where they held revival services. On one occasion, they awakened to find their host reading a book by a lamp stand in their bedroom. And there were other unbelievable stories—of finding bedbugs in their beds; of having no door on the bedroom and sometimes finding a child staring at them from the side of their bed; of beds that sank in the middle so their heads raised up on one end, and their feet raised up on the other; of driving through flooded areas to get to a meeting in another city; of paychecks that were often too small—and in one instance, not at all; and of putting chains on their car tires so they could drive on snowbound roads from one state to another.

During their last four years as evangelists, I traveled with them. Although quite small, I remember some of those adventures, like the one where the water was up to the car's running board as we crossed a flood in Oklahoma to get to Texas and my being so sick while traveling in New Mexico that Dad made sure I had the toy I wanted to help soothe the medicine going down.

It was customary for Mother to leave me on the front pew while she stepped on the platform to sing with Dad. During one of their services, when I was about two years old, Mom and Dad were singing a rather moving song when they noticed that the people of the congregation were smiling at one another. It wasn't until their eyes fell on the front row that they realized why everyone was tickled. To Mother's horrified eyes, I had taken off every stitch of clothing. There I was, as naked as a jaybird. (That is one memory I don't have, thank goodness!)

For nine years, they traveled, never knowing what they would find, all the while trusting in the belief that they were making a difference in the lives of countless men and women. Indeed, they did!

In 1969, while my brother, Paul, was stationed with the air force in the Philippines, he and one of his air force buddies decided to attend church at the Nazarene Mission Church in Angeles City. During the service, the pastor introduced Paul and his friend by name.

After the service ended and Paul was about to leave to go back to the base, he was approached by a couple who were members of that congregation. They inquired if Paul's dad was John Rhame, who had been an evangelist at one time. When Paul said yes, they shared that they both had been converted in one of Dad and Mom's meetings many years prior. Talk about surprise! Paul was eight thousand miles from the United States, yet he met a couple who had been saved under our parents' ministry. The stories Paul heard of their evangelistic travels in the late 1930s and early '40s were a testimony that they definitely had made a difference.

8

Pastoring a Church Has Its Rewards and Challenges, Even with a Roast

THE YEAR WAS 1944, AND Dad and Mother had been asked by Florida's district superintendent to come to Sebring, Florida, to establish, build, and pastor a brand new church. There would be only a handful of believers: eight adults and five children to be exact. The nation was at war, and the country was in distress. Commodities were hard to come by, and people were making sacrifices throughout America. Almost everything was in limited supply, including gas, time, and money. After praying and talking it over, they decided to accept the challenge and move to this picturesque town, leaving behind a slate of revival meetings they were to hold that extended three years. They met with the small group of excited believers, who had heard Dad preach in a tent revival and wanted him to be their first pastor. Together, they adopted a plan of action. For several months, the little band of members met in a small building to worship, pray, fast, and seek God's direction in finding a location, while the three of us lived in a boarding house.

It was not long before a miracle took place. On the corner of one of the busiest intersections in Sebring stood a Standard Oil service station, owned by Mr. Joe Stiles. He felt led to offer the property for ten dollars, an unbelievable price, plus the cost of removing two large storage tanks. What a wonderful location it was! Now, they were ready for the local architect to draw up plans. It was confirmation that the new direction in their lives was part of God's plan.

With low incomes, no equity, and a congregation too new to have any credit rating, they led the charge in their commitment to be obedient in what they believed God wanted for this city. It was agreed to be pay-as-you-go.

In order to obtain the materials necessary to build the church, Dad had to send a priority letter to Washington, DC, requesting permission to obtain the materials. After anxiously waiting, approval was given, and the plans for the building were ready to go. The first thing they did was remove the large gas storage tanks. Devoted volunteers gathered the necessary supplies to build the new church, step by step. Often, I would see Dad haul a load of concrete blocks in the trunk of his car, and he would join the others in laying them. Mother continued making a home for us at the boarding house while an attached parsonage to the church was being built.

Money began coming in, slowly at first, but then more people joined the church. At the end of fourteen months, a beautiful church and parsonage had been constructed. The Gothic stained-glass window that covered the front of the church was one of its outstanding architectural features. The real beauty, however, was found in the faithfulness of Dad, Mother, and this small and dedicated congregation.

The building was totally paid for by the Sunday when it was ready for worship. On that Sunday, two hundred people were seated in the sanctuary, with two hundred more standing in and outside the church. The church was known as the "miracle church." God blessed this new direction and Dad and Mother's call into the pastorate.

Dad had been used to traveling from the time he was a teenager, so it was not very long before he felt his work was complete, and it was time for him to move on to another pastorate. One of his members was so bent on Dad's staying that he offered Dad several acres of a productive orange grove if Dad wouldn't leave. In his young mind, Dad reasoned this was a temptation that should be avoided and declined the offer. Years later, we joked as he recalled the incident and lamented that he lacked the wisdom to accept and stay. When he served a church, he was not interested in making money—a good thing in this vocation. (They didn't ask me when the offer was made; I was too young.)

A few months later, they accepted a call to serve a church in Miami. While there, for our living quarters were a Sunday school classroom, with a small adjoining classroom serving as a kitchen. It took eighteen months for the men of the congregation to build a new parsonage. During that time, Mom cooked on a small gas stove and washed our clothes on a washboard. Even though she may have wanted to complain, I did not hear Mother complain even one time during those long months of waiting—not once! This was the way it had been for her entire life. She had the uncanny ability to put her needs behind her for the good of others and the church. During this time, Mother had several miscarriages, but still, she did not complain.

We had just settled in the new parsonage when southern Florida was hit by a hurricane that affected Miami. The parsonage was down in a little valley, and water flooded our yard. Dad and Mother burned lanterns when we lost electricity. Thousands of tadpoles and frogs turned up, croaking throughout the night, and scorpions took residence under beds and in our socks. The only way I could use the bathroom at night was to have Dad carry me so I would not be stung, which was extremely painful. In the light of day, we could see large coconut trees lining the street, and when it was safe to go outside, I thought it fun to climb on them to retrieve a coconut.

My grandfather Rhame had died before I was born, so I only knew my grandmother Rhame. She came to stay with us for several months, and during that time, she fell and broke her hip. Dad had his hands full—Mother was now pregnant with my brother, his own mother was in desperate need of care, and he had a church to pastor. The medication that my grandmother was taking after surgery caused her to have panic attacks. Every time Dad tried to carry her to the bathroom, she would hang on to the door jamb and yell for help. With everything else going on, this only added to a stressful situation.

After Grandmother healed to the point that she could return to her home in Ashville, North Carolina, and two months after my brother was born, Dad received a call to take a pastorate in Syracuse, New York. The fact that Syracuse was interested in a Southern minister intrigued Dad; that, along with the fine reputation of the church, inspired him to accept the call.

While Dad was busy with the demands of a church, mother set up housekeeping and purchased a roasting pot. Over the years, the roasting pot became one of her favorite utensils, and she seared literally hundreds of roasts as she welcomed guests to her table, including special church speakers, newlyweds, med students and their wives with little cash flow, and a host of friends and family members.

My children liked my roasts, but there was something special about their grandmother's roast. The same could be said for my brother's family, even though my sister-in-law is an excellent cook as well.

It was the leftover roast beef sandwiches that helped to win the heart of Bob, a singing cowboy and radio personality known as the Nightherder, and it was, of all places, in Syracuse, New York, where we were making our home. As an accomplished guitarist, Bob would often come to church on Sunday evenings, especially on nights when Dad would give in to pressure and play for the evening service, an occasion to which we all looked forward. Bringing his guitar with him, Bob loved to be invited to our home to jam with Dad after the evening service.

While Dad and this young man were playing their instruments, Mother would warm up the leftover roast beef from lunch and make the most wonderful sandwiches. To this day, I still can almost taste the flavor of those sandwiches. During those times of playing and visiting together, Bob became very interested in knowing more about Dad's life when he was in the entertainment field and also more about his faith. Mother's willingness to open up her home again, after a busy Sunday, played an influential role in the friendship that developed between Bob and Dad. In due time, Bob knelt at an altar of prayer and surrendered his life to the Lord.

Soon, he began bringing other young men, who lived on neighboring farms, to the evening services. Knowing they would be in the service, Dad would sometimes bring his guitar and play to their enjoyment. At their pleas, Dad sometimes ventured out and added one or more of the old tricks he had used when he was in the entertainment field. Dad was game for anything if it would win young men to Christ, even if it meant playing the guitar behind his back, over his shoulder, or—to Mother's not-so-sure approval—with his toes. (With Dad's love for entertaining but Mother's propensity for proper conduct, the fact that I never saw him do this again shows the weight she pulled in such matters.) As a teenager, I loved Dad's antics, because our church filled with teenage boys, all eager to see what this eclectic minister was going to do next.

Another of Dad's endearing features was his uncanny ability to memorize each of his three weekly sermons. He was a constant learner and observer of human nature and kept his sermons to thirty minutes, believing that the brain would only take in what the seat could endure, which was quite appealing to the teenagers in the services. In fact, his congregations became so spoiled that when long-winded guest speakers came to preach, I could see the squirming begin when they went over Dad's prescribed time limit.

Soon, the teenage boys joined our church's basketball team and began winning one game after another. By the end of the season, they were scheduled to play for the championship against another church at Syracuse's War Memorial, where they would be the opener for NBA's Syracuse Nationals game. Knowing how important good advertisement was, Dad opted not to allow a good opportunity to go by—he was ingenious enough to have shirts made for the players with the name of the church on their backs. The year was 1955, and the Syracuse Nationals won the NBA championship. Although this generated a great amount of hoopla and enthusiasm, it paled in significance to the enthusiasm Dad felt when one of these young men would give his heart to the Lord at the close of one of his messages.

As Mother did so often, she continued entertaining by opening the parsonage to members and guests. One occasion I remember so well was Mom's opening up the parsonage to feed the Eastern Nazarene College choir. The choir had to alter its schedule at the last minute and asked to sing for our morning worship service, instead of for the original church in which they were scheduled to sing. Mom knew the college students would need a place to eat after the worship service, so she set about organizing our home and the menu.

With the help of volunteer women in the church, she had enough food to feed the entire choir. How exciting for me—a young teenager with a house full of college students. I can still see them sitting at card tables in our large foyer, living room, music room, on the stairs of our two-story parsonage, on its landing, and at the dining room table. When it was over and the parsonage put back in place, Mom went again to the evening service. I think I would have taken a long nap and stayed there for the rest of the evening, but not Mom. She was out the door, in case she was needed.

As the damp winter months began to take their toll on Dad's health, the realization that he must make a change began to dawn on him and Mother. On many Sundays, he would stand before his congregation, even though he was running a high fever and had a throat so sore it was painful to speak. Finally, the doctor advised Dad that he needed to move to a warmer climate. As much as he and Mother wanted to stay, after eight years of pastoring a congregation who loved them and one they loved deeply, the decision was made—they left with sad hearts to pastor a church in Memphis, Tennessee, a city to which Mother had said she would never move as a pastor's wife. She learned never to say *never* after that move and came to serve and love other congregations in various pastorates. As with any vocation where people are involved, a pastorate is not without its own set of challenges. It can be quite frustrating, but at other times, it can be humorous.

One Sunday morning in Syracuse, Dad's message was on the sanctifying power of the Holy Spirit, what this meant, and how the Holy Spirit had walked with him in a personal relationship throughout the years since he gave his heart to the Lord.

In preaching on this subject, Dad shared the experience he had faced as a new Christian, right after he was converted in Gladewater, Texas. He told about the man who had almost sideswiped him as he was crossing the man's driveway and how he had been so angry that he had threatened to punch the guy. The sobering episode had made him realize his need for the guidance and the discipline of the Holy Spirit to become more Christlike in every area of his Christian walk, even in the way he responded to those "extra grace required" (abbreviated as "EGR") individuals.

After the day ended and we all were in bed, the phone rang at two o'clock in the morning. Generally, no one called in the middle of the night—especially not those who knew Dad and his inability to return to sleep once awakened— unless it was an emergency. When Dad answered the phone, a woman who had been in the congregation that morning said, "Pastor Rhame, I wanted to see how you answered the phone in the middle of the night—if you were still sanctified."

Dad was kind, even though he was not very happy. Little did the woman know that she had become one of those EGR members! Believe it or not, even after the phone call, she was a recipient of one of Mother's roasts. Nevertheless, what was an irritation that night became one of our favorite funny memories. As an adult married woman, I sometimes called Dad and asked if he was still sanctified, to which I always received a quick-witted response.

One of my other favorite stories from Syracuse had to do with Dad's black clerical collar, which he wore around his neck with either a black or gray suit. Catholic priests wore black collars with a black suit, while Protestant ministers generally wore black collars with gray suits. Generally, all wore clerical collars with their suits when on call. Since the majority of police officers were Catholic, if Dad was in a hurry, he would don his black clerical collar with his black suit. Every time he wore that combination and was pulled over for driving too fast, the police officer would look at Dad's attire and say, "Father, I am so sorry. Please continue where you are going." With that, the officer would walk back to his patrol car and drive away. With a smile, Dad wore that combination more and more when he was in a hurry.

Several years later in another pastorate, during a Wednesday evening prayer service, a woman raised her hand for prayer on behalf of a friend who was having marital problems caused by another woman. Of course, Dad included her friend in his special prayer that evening. Later that night, he found out that the prayer had been for a woman on the television soap opera, *As the World Turns*. Since neither he nor Mother watched the soaps, they had no idea that this was just an actress. This poor parishioner was so seriously involved in the TV program that she had completely detached herself from reality, was living out this program, and felt the character's marital discord needed prayer. Dad really was duped on that one.

Then there was the woman in one of Dad's earlier pastorates who decided to bawl out Mother in the vestibule after church. For some reason, this woman was very upset. I was a young girl at the time, but I remember watching Mother cry, and I became so angry. Later that night, as I replayed that scene in my mind before going to sleep, I thought of several ways to physically get rid of the woman. I only knew that she had hurt my mother, and that was all that mattered.

In one congregation, a wealthy oilman was so intent on running the church and showing off his power that he wanted Dad to hang a plaque in the church with the names of the highest financial contributors—with his name at the top. Dad refused to allow this to happen, which caused quite a stir with the man. From that time on, the man didn't hide the fact that he didn't like Dad.

In another congregation, a board member called a secret meeting without Dad's knowledge—a pastor is the head of the church board—to discuss one of the church members. Dad found out about the meeting, and when he showed up, the board member was embarrassed and angry. The immediate situation was diffused, but not without there being strained feelings from the man.

At the close of a service in another church, as Dad was by the door shaking hands with members and visitors, one of the men stopped to berate Dad, as he had opposed Dad's message that morning. Dad let him fume and fuss, while he remained silent. This man did not know how Dad had reined in his temper, but Dad's silence in the face of an angry accusation did more than a thousand words of defense. Within the week, this man came to Dad's office to apologize for his behavior and ask for prayer. There is something about a man praying with his pastor that brings restoration. From that time on, they became very good friends, and he and his wife shared several of Mother's great roasts at the parsonage.

For every challenge that Dad and Mother faced with irrational members, there are hundreds of wonderful stories that accompanied each pastorate. Thank goodness for all the positive and godly members in those congregations.

As I wrote this story, so many memories flooded my mind—memories of a man not only devoted to his faith but to his family. When Paul arrived from St. Louis to look over what I had written, he and I laughed as we once again thought about Dad's sense of humor, Mother's predictable reactions, and the funny things that we brought to the parsonage life.

When I was ten and eleven, I felt bad for Dad if he offered an altar invitation to those who may have needed to pray, and no one came. So I would walk down the aisle to the altar to pray. In my young mind, I reasoned that Dad's message must have been a failure, and I didn't want him to feel discouraged. In doing so, I probably gave my heart to the Lord dozens of times throughout my early adolescent years.

One Sunday, Paul and I were bickering with one another at the conclusion of the service. I don't know what possessed me, but just as he walked out on to the lawn, I decided to tackle him. I was an older teenager, and this was not a ladylike action. As Mother and church members were walking out of the church, there we were, wrestling on the ground. I can still hear Mother's horrified voice, yelling at us to stop. Of course, by that time we were laughing. Mother didn't think it was too funny, but we did, after seeing her face

Throughout the years, Dad never lost his love of boxing. When my brother was old enough, Dad and Paul would watch boxing matches on television after the Wednesday night service to see who would win the fight for that night. As soon as Friday night arrived, the two of them could be found watching another fight on television, which Dad thoroughly enjoyed.

When Paul became a teenager, he could coax Dad into sparring with him and his teenage buddies. In his boxing days, Dad would score points and knockdowns, with no one landing a single punch on him. Dad still had lightning-fast hands. Those times of sparring with Paul and his friends were special for Dad. Paul's friends would say in jest that Dad was a kind, gentle, and Christian man, but when he put on the gloves, he was Johnny Rhame again.

9

They Will Bear Fruit in Old Age—Psalm 92:14

THROUGHOUT THEIR YEARS OF MINISTRY, Mom and Dad would also be called to serve in Alabama, Texas, Missouri, and Arizona. Over several decades, they were a positive force in so many lives. One man who had been influenced by Dad wrote an article, telling how literally thousands of individuals had been inspired by Dad's life story. And by his side, as his partner in life and ministry, stood Mom, encouraging and helping to smooth out the rough spots in their human imperfections. In several churches, she became the pianist for the congregation, taught Sunday school classes, worked with mission and youth, and served wherever she was needed.

In the early part of his ministry, Dad graduated from a prescribed four-year course of study offered by the Nazarene denomination. He was also president of different ministerial alliances and served as chaplain while he was a captain in the civil air patrol (an official auxiliary of the United States Air Force), as well as serving as chaplain for different hospitals. He was elected to various district church boards, helped to organize several other churches while serving his own congregation, and was host pastor for radio broadcasts. He also continued playing for church audiences and taught several others how to play the guitar.

At one time, he was offered an honorary doctorate degree but turned it down, as he didn't feel he had rightfully earned it. His energy and love for and with people of all races, cultures, and socioeconomic status was evidenced by the letters and cards he received throughout his lifetime. He was one of the first evangelists to engage a black singer to join him in one of his meetings—huge for that time, especially since he had Southern roots. On two other occasions as pastor, he invited women to hold revivals for him in Syracuse in the '50s. I was honored to be asked to speak in his morning service in Phoenix, Arizona, in the early '70s. In many ways, he was ahead of his time.

Their last pastorate was in Peoria, Arizona, right outside of Phoenix. The church's congregation, the weather, and the opportunities to play golf each week made for an ideal situation for Dad. After serving for several years and feeling that he needed to retire and let someone younger take his place, he announced his intentions to the congregation—he was planning to move to Cape Girardeau, Missouri, where Paul's and my families lived. Again, as before in Sebring so many years prior, an enticement to stay was offered. This time, however, instead of an orange grove, one of his members offered to build him a home if he would retire in Peoria. The proposal was very tempting, but as a family, we all agreed that his and Mom's moving closer to our homes would be the wise thing to do in their retirement. With mixed emotions, they moved all their belongings to a cozy home in Cape Girardeau in 1976.

Dad tried to go back into the evangelistic field, but times had changed, and Mother, after traveling with him to one church, decided this lifestyle was no longer for her. She was not the young girl of years ago and no longer wanted to travel. When he went to his next engagement, it was not the same. In two of his letters to her, he wrote the news of the revivals and that he missed her terribly. I have chosen a couple of excerpts. With each letter, Dad always told Mom of his love for her and would close by including other members of the family, sometimes with the sense of humor for which he was noted.

Dear Sweetheart,

All the way up here I had the feeling that I had forgotten something. Every service station, every restaurant, and at the motel, I double-checked three times. Then I finally realized why I felt that way. You were not with me. I have really missed you. I love you more than ever.

Tell Paul, Jana, Ted, Carolyn, Greg, and Laurie hello.

Your big brown-eyed baby,
John

Dear Sweetheart,

I plan to play the other two songs Sunday. ... It does not take the place of having you with me. I miss you so much.

This will most probably be my last letter from here. Give all my love to Carolyn, Gregory, Jana, Laurie, Paul, and Ted.

I placed them in alphabetical order so as to avoid the possibility of discrimination.

Love,
John

The culture of the 1970s and '80s was far different from the culture of the '30s and early '40s. Not only was Mother absent, but churches were no longer holding weeklong revival meetings. Most had gone to weekends or Sunday-to-Wednesday revivals. Many of the pastors Dad knew had retired. After so many years serving as a pastor, his name was no longer recognized as it had been many years earlier. Young, energetic evangelists were taking over the speaking engagements. It came as a huge disappointment to him. Finally, he resigned himself to the change and returned to his home, leaving this renewed dream behind.

For the next several years, he helped the pastor of Cape Girardeau's Nazarene church by calling on shut-ins, visiting nursing homes and hospitals, sharing his musical talent, teaching guitar lessons, and filling in the pulpit when needed. It was on a walk to the hospital to call on a member that he was struck by a car and taken to the hospital with a broken arm. After the blow from the accident to his body, Dad began experiencing pain in his abdomen, and in a few months, our family learned that Dad had pancreatic cancer and had only a few months to live. This was the beginning of our taping interviews with him to preserve for our families. At one point, he was encouraged to write his life story but gave only a small portion of it in a booklet to give to his friends.

From the time he was spiritually born again and over the years that Dad walked with the Lord, there was no longer the violent temper. There was no bitterness for the father who had abused him and his sister. There was no self-serving aggrandizement as when he still played for audiences. Rather there was a man who, for fifty-three years, had served the Lord and others with humility, patience, love, forgiveness, and grace.

As Dad grew older, my friends would remark about the sweet spirit he always exuded. When I would share this with him, he would laugh and say, "You can grow older and be cranky, or you can grow older and mellow. I am so mellow now that I am downright rotten."

During the final days before the Lord called Dad home to be with Him, Mother slept on the floor beside his bed to keep him from getting up and falling. My brother drove in from St. Louis, where he now was living, on several occasions to be by his side. Paul was a very good guitarist, so he would pick up Dad's guitar and sing one of his favorite songs, *Just a Closer Walk with Thee*, over and over, to Dad's repeated requests. I would read one of his favorite passages, found in Psalm 91:1–2. "He who dwells in the secret place of the Most High shall abide under the shadow of the Almighty. I will say of the Lord, He is my refuge and my fortress: My God, in Him I will trust" (NIV).

On July 9, 1986, Dad passed to the other side—a man totally fulfilled. He died only a few weeks before he and Mother were to celebrate their fiftieth wedding anniversary, an anniversary he had fought hard to celebrate.

Dad's close friend and golfing partner, Rev. Renard Smith, who also had been his former district superintendent in Syracuse, had flown into Cape Girardeau to visit and encourage him. When it was time for Reverend Smith to depart, the two hugged one another and wept as they said their last good-byes. As Renard walked to the door, his parting words were, "When you get to heaven, wait for me at the ninth hole." I have a feeling that when Renard went to heaven, Dad was waiting. To Mom's added surprise and after so many years, cards and letters full of remembrance of Dad's influence and love were sent to Mom from across the nation. His life had not been in vain, even in death.

One of his favorite passages is found in Matthew 6:19, which reads, "Lay not up for yourselves treasures upon earth, where moth and rust doth corrupt, and where thieves break through and steal: But lay up for yourselves treasures in heaven, where neither moth nor rust doth corrupt, and thieves do not break in and steal. For where your treasure is, there your heart will be also" (NKJV).

If anyone had asked him if the sacrifice of fame and fortune was worth it, I imagine he would have smiled and said yes. His wealth was not on this earth; instead, he stored up eternal treasures in heaven.

After Dad's death, Mother was lonely but continued to serve others by taking food to her neighbors and to church members who were ill, visiting nursing homes and homebound friends, playing the piano for worship service when needed, and volunteering at one of the local hospitals for several years. She also set up a scholarship at Nazarene Bible College, a four-year college in Colorado Springs, Colorado, for the exclusive task of preparing ministers.

With Paul and Jana living in St. Louis, and Ted and me now living in Little Rock, the time came when we did not feel it safe for Mom to live alone. Her eyesight was failing. In February 2004, she moved to my home in Little Rock.

Both the pastor at Calvary's Church of the Nazarene, Rodney Shanner, and my pastor at Parkway Place Baptist Church, Allan Greer, spent time with Mom. Pastor Greer often referred to her as "Gram," a name given to her by our families, and Reverend Shanner made sure she had another Outstanding Service award from the Nazarene headquarters. Denominations held no boundaries, and for that, I am most appreciative.

By 2010, Mother had experienced several mini-stokes that left her unable to chew her food and swallow properly. Unable to speak with clarity, she wrote notes to all of us, telling us of her love and her walk with the Lord. Even with all her health issues, she managed to keep her sense of humor. Often, she would teasingly write, "I love all my grandchildren, even Tim" (Paul's son) or "even Greg" (my son). She couldn't wait to get a response and would shake her shoulders, trying hard to laugh. She and my son-in-law Mike would banter back and forth, and she included him on that list as well.

In the fall of that year, it became evident that Ted and I no longer could give Mom the care she needed so desperately. With overwhelming sadness on our part and hers, we and Paul made the decision to place her in the Baptist Health Center, a very nice nursing home. There, she wrote to all the residents about her life with Dad in the evangelistic field, and always she wrote of her love for our families. In time, she could no longer see or speak. In August 2012, while standing by her side, with her hand in mine, and with my daughters, Laurie and Sarah, by my side, she died peacefully, knowing that her life had been filled with God's purpose.

Her funeral was in Cape Girardeau, where Dad was buried, and I was surprised that so many came to offer their condolences and tell of their love for her and for Dad, even though she had been gone from that city for more than eleven years. My son, Greg, now a pastor, officiated at her funeral, while our family shared funny and precious memories of her life, making it a celebration of her homecoming to be with the Lord. A year after she had died, I heard from a nurse who said that those who had known Mom at the nursing home still talked about her gracious and sweet spirit.

Dad and Mother were buried in the same grave, with her casket on top of his. A beautifully engraved metal medallion is fastened on the headstone, in the center of which is the inscription *Minister*, and surrounding that word is *Church of the Nazarene*, where both served for so many years. Each had received the highest award given by their denomination, an Outstanding Distinguished award. Second Timothy 4:7–9 reads, "I have fought the good fight, I have finished the race, I have kept the faith. Now there is in store for me the crown of righteousness, which the Lord, the righteous Judge, will award to me on that day— and not only to me, but also to all who have longed for his appearing" (NKJV).

Dad, you fought another fight. This time it was in keeping the faith that you embraced so many years ago. You finished the race that you ran. You added Mom to the mix, and both of you served with distinction. You are wearing your crowns. What a joy to know that all you both did was not in vain. We are planning on seeing you someday, by holding on to God's promise.

Afterword

SINCE PROFESSIONAL COUNSELING WAS PROBABLY not available to Dad as a young man, he was fortunate that godly men of character, integrity, wisdom, and a love for the Lord took the time to listen and offer guidance when he became a new believer. They became Dad's mentors, encouraging him and offering needed support. Even with the healing that can come from the Holy Spirit, I am certain that these men played a significant role in the healing process of overwhelming emotions that lingered from the psychological and physical abuse at the hands of his alcoholic father. And why shouldn't it? One doesn't forget that kind of abuse overnight. Those feelings would certainly explain the tremendous anger he felt before he became a Christian and the nervousness that lingered with him all his life. Even though he was not privileged to have professional counseling, I always admired him for the insight God gave in this area and for the men who stood by his side during those early years.

For one thing, he never allowed bitterness to well up and destroy his joy. A few years before his father died, Dad had forgiven him in his heart. By this time, he and Mother were married, and, with Mother standing by his side, he shared what meager income they had managed to earn as evangelists to assist in my grandfather's medical bills. Dad continue to help his mother financially until she, too, passed from this earth. He had honored his parents, even though he had painful memories. There is something to be said for how God can change the heart.

Dad believed that living in the past and continuously rehashing hurts only served to defeat. Neither Paul nor I remember his sharing what had happened to him as a child. The only time he spoke of this was in sharing his life story from the pulpit with various congregations. His purpose in retelling his story of redemption—from the time he was a prizefighter and professional entertainer to the day he became a born-again Christian—was to help others find hope and strength in facing similar trials and hardships. He wanted others to experience the same wholeness he had found. Dad knew that bitterness and resentment only served to harm the individual who held on to these emotions.

I also admired Dad's sensitivity to addiction. He knew that there were those with addictive behavior who might continuously struggle in this area. Today, our society faces other forms of addiction—harmful drugs of all kind, pornography, and various sexual addictions, just to name a few. His own experience was a difficult time in his life. He was always mentoring, encouraging, and praying with those who were dealing with harmful addictions. He did not try to clean them up before they accepted Christ as their personal Savior. That was God's job. First John 1:9 reads, "If we confess our sins, He is faithful and just to forgive us our sins and to cleanse us from all unrighteousness" (NIV). It was Dad's job to present that gospel and to assist in the growth of these individuals who were still struggling with addiction. From my personal perspective, I believe that Dad's willingness to surrender everything to the Lord, no matter the cost, was part of the healing answer to his addiction. He also consistently took time every day to pray and get into God's Word. Faith, with discipline, can go a long way.

Dad believed that the goal of a Christian should be to display love and grace in his or her daily walk. The walk had to go farther than just talking about being a

Christ-follower. As I mentioned, in his teen years, Dad's seeing a man profess to be a Christian while engaging in drunkenness turned Dad off to any religion. He learned later to discern those who were merely talking the talk and encouraged others to keep their eyes on God and not man. Certainly, this is easier said than done but is necessary to keep the faith.

He was also very generous, often giving from his pocket when his pockets were not full. I never heard him say that his goal was to become wealthy. He believed that true wealth came from sources other than worldly goods. From the time he became a Christian to the time of his death, he gave to others, even when in the evangelistic field, when he and Mother sometimes had very little.

Dad was not a perfect man. There has only been one man who walked this earth who could proclaim that role. When Dad understood an area of weakness, he was open to working on that area, with the help of the Holy Spirit. He didn't carry the attitude of "That's the way I am; live with it." He was always striving to become a better person. I have tried to live by that motto, and heaven only knows, I have needed God's help.

I wish all my readers could have known him. He was as quick-witted in his sermons as he was as an entertainer. He believed in laughter and brushed aside any legalism that could discourage a person from following Christ Jesus. His messages were spot-on, rather than about how many rules we should follow.

I thank you for taking the time to read Dad's story. My prayer is that his story will capture what it means to journey throughout life with a faith so real and persuasive that you will seek a closer walk with the Lord. May God continue to bless and use this story for years to come.

CPSIA information can be obtained
at www.ICGtesting.com
Printed in the USA
FFOW04n2137210216
21706FF

9 781512 727449